Theory of Music Grade 5
November 2019

Instructions to Candidates

1. The time allowed for answering this paper is **three (3) hours.**
2. Fill in your name and the candidate number printed on your appointment form in the appropriate spaces on this paper, and on any other sheets that you use.
3. **Do not open this paper until you are told to do so.**
4. This paper contains **seven (7) sections** and you should answer all of them.
5. Read each question carefully before answering it. Your answers must be written legibly in pen or pencil in the spaces provided.
6. You are reminded that you are bound by the regulations for written exams displayed at the exam centre and listed on page 4 of the current edition of the written exams syllabus. In particular, you are reminded that you are not allowed to bring books, music or papers into the exam room. Bags must be left at the back of the room under the supervision of the invigilator.
7. If you leave the exam room you will not be allowed to return.

(C-05)

Section 1 (10 marks)

Boxes
exami
use o

Put a tick (✓) in the box next to the correct answer.

Example

Name this note:

A ☐   D ☐   C ☑

This shows that you think **C** is the correct answer.

1.1   Name the circled note:

E ☐   F# ☐   G ☐

1.2   Which rest(s) should be put below the asterisk (*) to complete the bar?

1.3   Which is the correct time signature?

$\frac{12}{8}$ ☐ $\frac{3}{2}$ ☐ $\frac{5}{4}$ ☐

1.4   Which note is the enharmonic equivalent of this note?

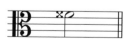

Gb ☐   G ☐   Ab ☑

1.5   Which note is the dominant of the minor key shown by this key signature?

E ☐   F ☐   F# ☐

Put a tick (✓) in the box next to the correct answer.

1.6   An **acciaccatura** is:

a grace note ☐
an accent ☐
an accidental ☐

1.7   The correct name for the following scale is:

F natural minor scale ascending ☐
F harmonic minor scale ascending ☐
F melodic minor scale ascending ☐

1.8   Which Roman numeral fits below this supertonic triad?

II ☐   ii ☐   IV ☐

1.9   Which of the following instruments sometimes uses this clef?

violin ☐   viola ☐   cello ☐

1.10   Name this cadence:

plagal cadence in D minor ☐
perfect cadence in D minor ☐
imperfect cadence in D minor ☐

(Please turn over for section 2)

Section 2 (15 marks)

Boxes
exami
use or

2.1 Write a one-octave C♯ melodic minor scale in crotchets, going down then up. Use a key signature.

2.2 Write the key signature of the key shown, then write its one-octave arpeggio in the rhythm given below.

Db major, going down then up

Section 3 (10 marks)

3.1 Circle five different mistakes in the following music, then write it out correctly.

4

Section 4 (15 marks)

4.1 Transpose this melody down a perfect 5th. Use a key signature.

Handel

Section 5 (15 marks)

5.1 Using crotchets, write out well-balanced 4-part chords for SATB using the chords shown by the Roman numerals below.

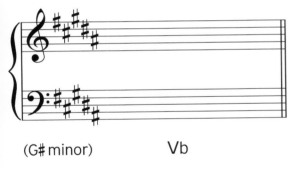

(G♯ minor)   Vb

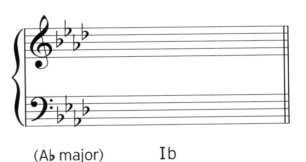

(A♭ major)   Ib

Section 6 (15 marks)

6.1 Use notes from the chords shown by the Roman numerals to write a tune above the bass line. Decorate your tune (eg with passing notes) once you have the main harmony notes in place.

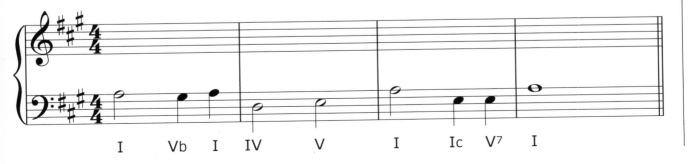

I   Vb   I   IV   V   I   Ic   V⁷   I

5

Section 7 (20 marks)

Boxe
exam
use o

Look at the following piece and answer the questions opposite.

7.1   What is the key at the start of this piece? _____

7.2   This piece does not begin on the first beat of the bar. What is the musical term for this?

_____

7.3   To which related key does the music modulate in bars 7 and 8? _____

7.4   Name the ornament used in bar 3 (treble part). _____

7.5   Circle an example of a dominant 7th chord in root position.

7.6   Is the sequence in bars 13 and 14 (treble part) real or tonal? _____

7.7   What is the form of this piece? _____

7.8   Name the interval between the two notes marked with asterisks (*) in bar 6 (bass part).

_____

7.9   Write appropriate Roman numerals below the chords on the second and third beats in bar 15 and the first beat in bar 16.

7.10   What cadence is formed by these chords? _____

Theory of Music Grade 5

November 2019

TRINITY
COLLEGE LONDON

Your full name (as on appointment form). Please use BLOCK CAPITALS.

_____

Your signature

_____

Candidate number

_____

Centre

_____

Instructions to Candidates

1. The time allowed for answering this paper is **three (3) hours.**
2. Fill in your name and the candidate number printed on your appointment form in the appropriate spaces on this paper, and on any other sheets that you use.
3. **Do not open this paper until you are told to do so.**
4. This paper contains **seven (7) sections** and you should answer all of them.
5. Read each question carefully before answering it. Your answers must be written legibly in pen or pencil in the spaces provided.
6. You are reminded that you are bound by the regulations for written exams displayed at the exam centre and listed on page 4 of the current edition of the written exams syllabus. In particular, you are reminded that you are not allowed to bring books, music or papers into the exam room. Bags must be left at the back of the room under the supervision of the invigilator.
7. If you leave the exam room you will not be allowed to return.

Examiner's use only:

1 (10)	
2 (15)	
3 (10)	
4 (15)	
5 (15)	
6 (15)	
7 (20)	
Total	

Section 1 (10 marks)

Put a tick (✓) in the box next to the correct answer.

Example

Name this note:

A ☐   D ☐   C ☑

This shows that you think **C** is the correct answer.

1.1   Name the circled note:

C♮ ☐   G♮ ☐   A♮ ☐

1.2   Which is the correct time signature?

$\frac{3}{2}$ ☐ $\frac{12}{8}$ ☐ $\frac{6}{4}$ ☐

1.3   Which rest(s) should be put below the asterisk (*) to complete the bar?

☐   ☐   ☐

1.4   Which note is the enharmonic equivalent of this note?

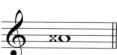

B♭ ☐   D♯ ☐   B♮ ☐

1.5   What does **con fuoco** mean:

with passion ☐
resolutely ☐
with fire ☐

2

Put a tick (✓) in the box next to the correct answer.

1.6   Which is the supertonic of the major key shown by this key signature?

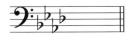

Ab ☐   Bb ☐   G ☐   ☐

1.7   Which of these ornaments should be played as follows:

tr ☐   ☐   ☐   ☐

1.8   Which Roman numeral fits below this subdominant triad?

iv ☐   IV ☐   ii ☐   ☐

1.9   The interval of a major 3rd when inverted becomes:

a major 6th ☐
an augmented 4th ☐
a minor 6th ☐   ☐

1.10   Name this cadence:

plagal cadence in B minor ☐
imperfect cadence in B minor ☐
perfect cadence in B minor ☐   ☐

(Please turn over for section 2)

Section 2 (15 marks)

Boxes for examiner use only

2.1   Write a one-octave G♯ melodic minor scale in crotchets, going down then up.
       Use a key signature and add any necessary accidentals.

2.2   Write the key signature of the key shown, then write its one-octave arpeggio in the rhythm
       given below.

       B major, going down then up

Section 3 (10 marks)

3.1   Circle five different mistakes in the following music, then write it out correctly.

Section 4 (15 marks)

4.1 Transpose this melody down a perfect 4th. Use a key signature.

Verdi

Section 5 (15 marks)

5.1 Using crotchets, write out well-balanced 4-part chords for SATB using the chords shown by the Roman numerals below.

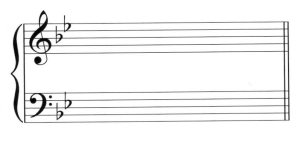

(G minor)   Vb

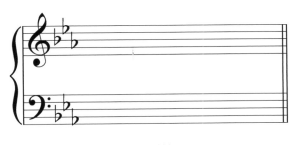

(E♭ major)   iib

Section 6 (15 marks)

6.1 Use notes from the chords shown by the chord symbols to write a tune above the bass line. Decorate your tune (eg with passing notes) once you have the main harmony notes in place.

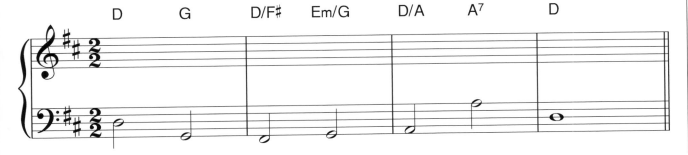

Section 7 (20 marks)

Look at the following piece and answer the questions opposite.

7.1   In which key is this piece? _____

7.2   Name a related key which has the same key signature: _____

7.3   Write an appropriate Roman numeral below the first beat of bar 6.

7.4   Look at the left-hand pattern in bars 3 and 4. What form of the minor scale is being used?

       _____

7.5   Name the interval marked with an asterisk (*) in bar 22 (right-hand).

       _____

7.6   Rewrite bars 34 and 35 (right-hand only) in the tenor clef. Remember to use a key signature.

7.7   Circle a lower auxiliary note in bar 3 (left-hand).

7.8   What does *sotto voce* mean? _____

7.9   Circle a dominant 7th chord.

7.10   Identify two types of articulation mark used in this piece and describe how they might be played.

       _____

       _____